MY WORLD OF SCIENCE

Sound and Hearing

Revised and Updated

Angela Royston

Heinemann
LIBRARY

www.heinemann.co.uk/library

Visit our website to find out more information about Heinemann Library books.

To order:
- ☏ Phone 44 (0) 1865 888066
- 🖹 Send a fax to 44 (0) 1865 314091
- 💻 Visit the Heinemann Bookshop at www.heinemann.co.uk/library to browse our catalogue and order online.

First published in Great Britain by Heinemann Library, Halley Court, Jordan Hill, Oxford OX2 8EJ, part of Pearson Education. Heinemann is a registered trademark of Pearson Education Ltd.

Editorial: Diyan Leake
Design: Joanna Hinton-Malivoire
Picture research: Melissa Allison and Mica Brancic
Production: Duncan Gilbert

Originated by Chroma Graphics (Overseas) Pte Ltd
Printed and bound in China by South China Printing Company Ltd

ISBN 978 0 431 13770 4 (hardback)
12 11 10 09 08
10 9 8 7 6 5 4 3 2 1

ISBN 978 0 431 13828 2 (paperback)
12 11 10 09 08
10 9 8 7 6 5 4 3 2 1

British Library Cataloguing in Publication Data
Royston, Angela
  Sound and hearing. – New ed. – (My world of science)
  1. Sound – Juvenile literature 2. Hearing – Juvenile literature
  I. Title
  534

Acknowledgements
The publishers would like to thank the following for permission to reproduce photographs: © Corbis p. **10** (Gavriel Jecan); © Eye Ubiquitous pp. **5** (G. Daniels), **8**, **28**; © Getty Images p. **26**; Robert Harding p. **22**; © Science Photo Library pp. **9** (Tim Davis), **12** (Jonathan Watts), **14** (Mark Burnett); © Stone pp. **13**, **18**; © Trevor Clifford pp. **7**, **15**, **16**, **17**, **19**, **21**, **23**, **24**, **27**, **29**; © Trip/H. Rogers pp. **4**, **6**, **11**, **20**, **25**.

Cover photograph reproduced with permission of © Photolibrary (fstop/Martin Diebel).

The publishers would like to thank Jon Bliss for his assistance in the preparation of this book.

Every effort has been made to contact copyright holders of any material reproduced in this book. Any omissions will be rectified in subsequent printings if notice is given to the publishers.

Contents

Any words appearing in the text in bold, **like this**, are explained in the glossary.

What is sound?

Sound is what we hear when something makes a noise. The dog in the picture is barking. People can hear the sounds a dog makes when it barks.

Sometimes you can hear many noises at the same time. The people in this street can hear the sound of traffic and the sound of people talking.

Making sounds

There are many different ways to make sounds. This father is shaking a rattle to make a noise. Banging, scraping, and rubbing also make sounds.

These children are all making sounds. Each child is making sounds in a different way. What is each one doing to make a sound? (Answer on page 31.)

Describing sounds

There are many words to describe how a noise sounds. These bells make a ringing sound. An alarm clock makes a different kind of ringing sound.

Spanish dancers sometimes use **castanets**. The dancer makes a clicking sound with the castanets. She makes a stomping sound with her feet.

castanets

Loud and soft

If you bang something hard, it will make a loud noise. If you just tap it, it will make a soft noise.

Cats purr when they are happy. *Purr* is a word that describes a soft sound. Some words describe loud sounds – for example, *shout*, *bang*, *roar*, and *clatter*.

Vibrations in the air

guitar string

When you **pluck** the string of a guitar, it moves back and forth very fast. This makes the air around it move fast, too. We say the air **vibrates**.

The vibrating air makes the sound. The **vibrations** move through the air like the ripples on a pond.

Ears and hearing

You hear sounds when **vibrations** in the air reach your ears. The vibrating air makes your **eardrums vibrate**. The vibrations pass inside your ears.

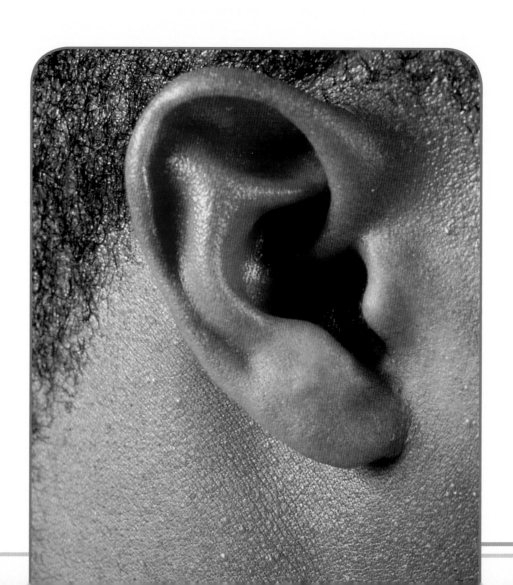

If you cover your ears with your hands, you cannot hear so well. This is because less moving air reaches your eardrums.

Talking

We can make sounds and talk because we have **vocal cords** in our throats. As you breathe out, the air makes the cords **vibrate**.

Put your hand on your throat and make a noise. You will feel your vocal cords vibrating. You make different sounds by moving your lips, tongue, and teeth.

Musical sounds

Instruments make air **vibrate** in different ways. Piano keys are joined to hammers inside the piano. When you press a key, a hammer hits a wire and makes it vibrate.

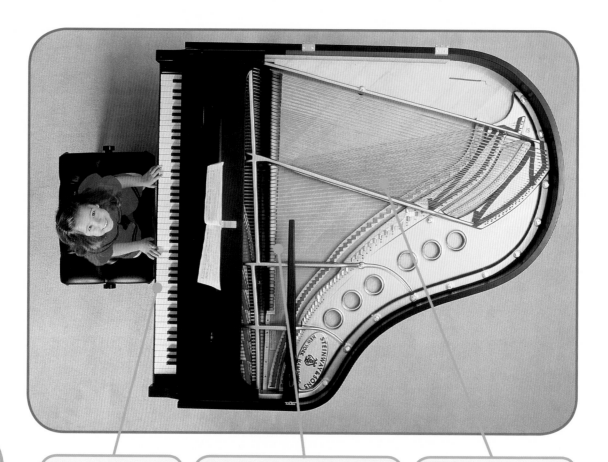

keys

hammers

wires

When you blow into a recorder or a trumpet, you make the air inside it vibrate. When you bang a drum, the part that you hit vibrates.

High and low

Musical instruments make many different notes. When you **pluck** a thin violin string, it makes a high note. A thick string makes a low note.

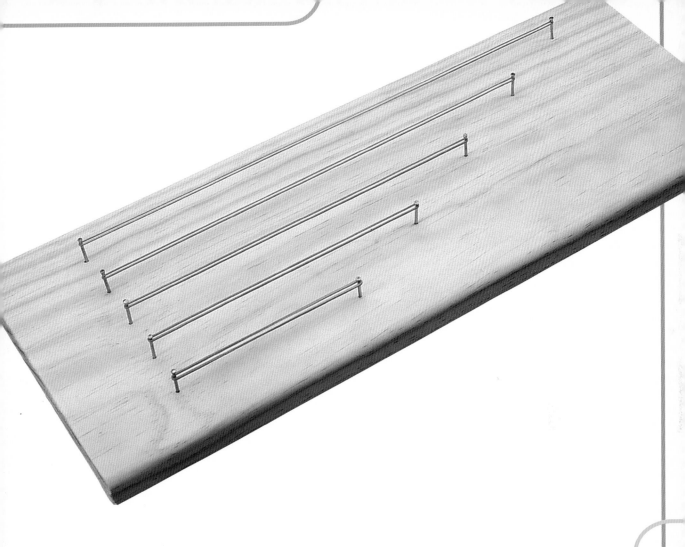

You can make your own instrument using rubber bands stretched between nails. Which rubber band do you think will make the highest note? (Answer on page 31.)

Sound travels

The closer you are to a sound, the louder it is. The noise of an aeroplane becomes quieter and fainter as it flies further away.

Pour a fizzy drink and listen. You will hear
the bubbles bursting. When you move
the glass away, the sounds no longer
reach your ear.

Hearing but not seeing

Sound can travel around corners and over things. You may be able to hear the sound, even if you cannot see who is making it.

Sound can travel through wood, water, and most other things. People inside a house may not be able to see who is knocking on the door, but they can hear them.

Where is it coming from?

We have two ears to help us hear where sound is coming from. When you cross the road, you must listen as well as look for traffic.

Turning your head can help you tell the direction of a sound. When you cannot see, you must listen hard for any noises.

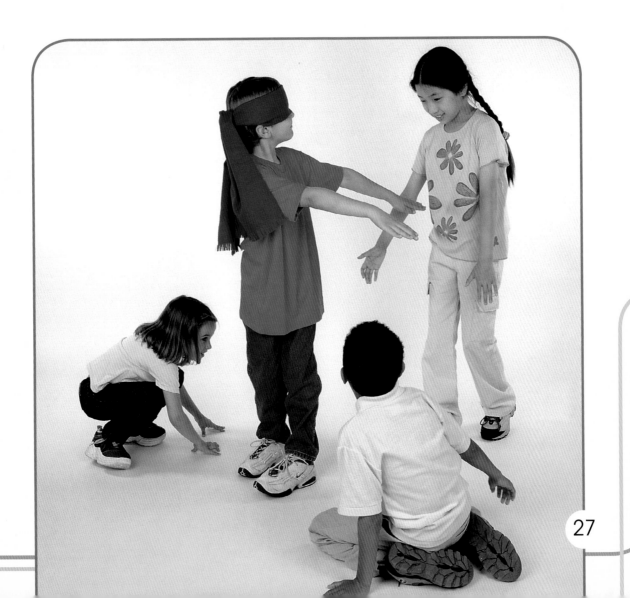

Dangerous sound

Very loud noises can **damage** the inside of your ears. If this happens, you may go **deaf**. People wear ear protectors to keep out the sound of loud noises.

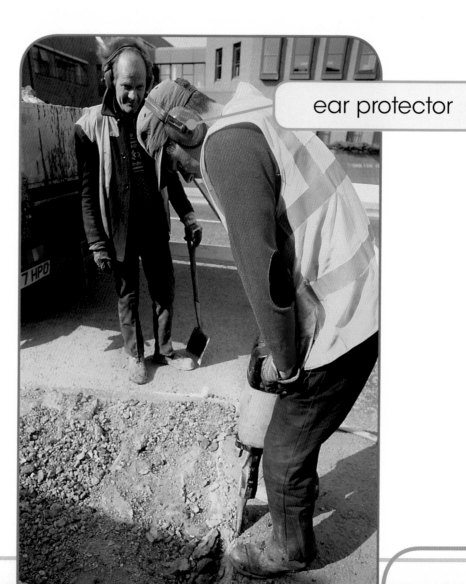

ear protector

If you listen to music through headphones, make sure the sound is not too loud. Look after your hearing so that you can hear for many years.

ELIN	
Z771858	
PETERS	23-Mar-2011
534	£10.99

Glossary

castanets two pieces of wood which are clicked together by the fingers

damage hurt or injure

deaf not able to hear

eardrum very thin sheet of skin in your ear

pluck pull strings with the fingers

vibrate move a small distance backwards and forwards very fast

vibration very fast movement backwards and forwards

vocal cords the two parts in your throat that vibrate when you speak or sing

Answers

Page 7 – The girl is tapping a drum. The boy on the left is plucking the strings of a guitar. The boy on the right is banging with a hammer.

Page 21 – The longest rubber band will make the highest note. This is because it is stretched thinner than any of the other rubber bands.

More books to read

The Best Ears in the World: A first look at sound and hearing, Claire Llewellyn (Hodder Wayland, 2002)

Sound: Listen Up! Wendy Sadler (Raintree, 2005)

Start-up Science: Sound and Hearing, Claire Llewellyn (Evans, 2004)

Index